Well today is Not a good day because CHLOE got ~~BiTE~~ Bit and the Car did Not Sorj

The Micik... BeTbe

The Micete paper BeThs

the Year
I Didn't Go
to
School

BY GISELLE POTTER

An Anne Schwartz Book
Atheneum Books for Young Readers
New York London Toronto Sydney Singapore

Atheneum Books for Young Readers
An imprint of Simon & Schuster Children's
Publishing Division
1230 Avenue of the Americas
New York, New York 10020

Book design by Ann Bobco
The text of this book is set in Gararond Medium.
The illustrations are rendered in pencil, ink gouache,
gesso, and watercolor.
Printed in Hong Kong
10 9 8 7 6 5 4 3 2 1
Library of Congress Cataloging-in-Publication Data
Potter, Giselle.
The year I didn't go to school / written and illustrated
by Giselle Potter.
p. cm.
"An Anne Schwartz book."
Summary: Relates the experience of children's author
Giselle Potter when, at the age of seven, she toured
Italy with her family's tiny theater company, The
Mystic Paper Beasts.
ISBN 0-689-84730-0
1. Potter, Giselle—Childhood and youth—
Juvenile literature. 2. Puppet theater—Italy—History—
20th century—Juvenile literature. 3. Authors,
American—20th century—Biography—Juvenile
literature. 4. Americans—Italy—History—20th
Century—Juvenile literature. 5. Potter, Giselle—
Journeys—Italy—Juvenile literature. 6. Italy—Social
life and customs—Juvenile literature. [1. Potter,
Giselle—Childhood and youth. 2. Puppet theater. 3.
Authors, American. 4. Italy—Social life and customs.]
I. Title.
Ps3566.O697 Z477 2002
818'.5403—dc21
[B]
2001046125

FIRST
EDITION

AUTHOR'S NOTE

When I was three years old, my parents started a puppet theater company named "The Mystic Paper Beasts"—"Mystic" partly after Mystic, Connecticut, the town where it all began, and "Paper Beasts" because we made our masks and puppets out of papier-mâché. My dad sculpted, and Mom painted. Sometimes I helped her. After a few years of performing with friends, Mom and Dad decided it would be easier to have a family troupe . . . and the four of us went on tour. We went to Italy—a place far from Mystic—and I kept a journal about all of our adventures. (You can see some of it on the endpapers of this book.)

When I was eighteen, my parents got divorced and my sister, Chloë, and I weren't living at home anymore, so the family theater ended. But to this day, my dad and his wife, Marya, continue to perform with their own version of The Mystic Paper Beasts. I'm now married to Kier, who makes tiny carved wooden puppets . . . and sometimes I help with his performances.

WhEn I waS SEVEn, I didn't go to school

for a whole year. Instead I went away to Italy with my parents, my little sister Chloë, four huge steamer trunks filled with puppets, masks, and musical instruments, my stuffed panda Samantha, and a journal to keep track of all that happened. Our own tiny theater company, The Mystic Paper Beasts, was going on tour.

With a sad heart, I said good-bye to Alice and Fuller. They're my grandparents, but we've always called them by their real names. In the airport, Fuller danced a farewell dance, waving his hands like fluttering butterflies and springing from one slipper to another. I looked down at my shoes and swallowed the big lumps in my throat, so no one would know I was scared to go.

After a long plane ride we arrived in Italy, the country that's shaped like a boot. Tiny cars filled with big families zoomed every which way, big men drank coffee from tiny cups, and the air was full of new smells. At a market Mom bought us fruit all wrapped in pretty papers. I ate the fruit and saved the wrappers to glue in my journal later.

Meanwhile Dad loaded our trunks into an old wooden carnival truck he'd bought. We'd painted clouds, birds, and "The Mystic Paper Beasts" on the side of it.

At last, we were on our way. . . .

We did our first show in the middle of the bustling city of Florence.

D ad shouted:

"Hear ye, hear ye,

signore y signori

(ladies and gentlemen),

Vieni guardare un spettacolo in la piazza

(come see a play in the piazza)—

un circo Di maschera

(a circus of masks)

per tutti Le gente!

(for everyone!)"

He was a stork on stilts with Chloë on his shoulders, and I followed as a panda beating a drum.

While an audience gathered, Mom played some music that could make you dizzy, called a *tarantella*, on her accordion.

Suddenly, out of nowhere, two policemen marched right up and started scolding us in Italian. I held Chloë's hand and stood there pretending I wasn't scared, while Mom and Dad scurried around packing our trunks.

We didn't have a permit, and so we had to leave.

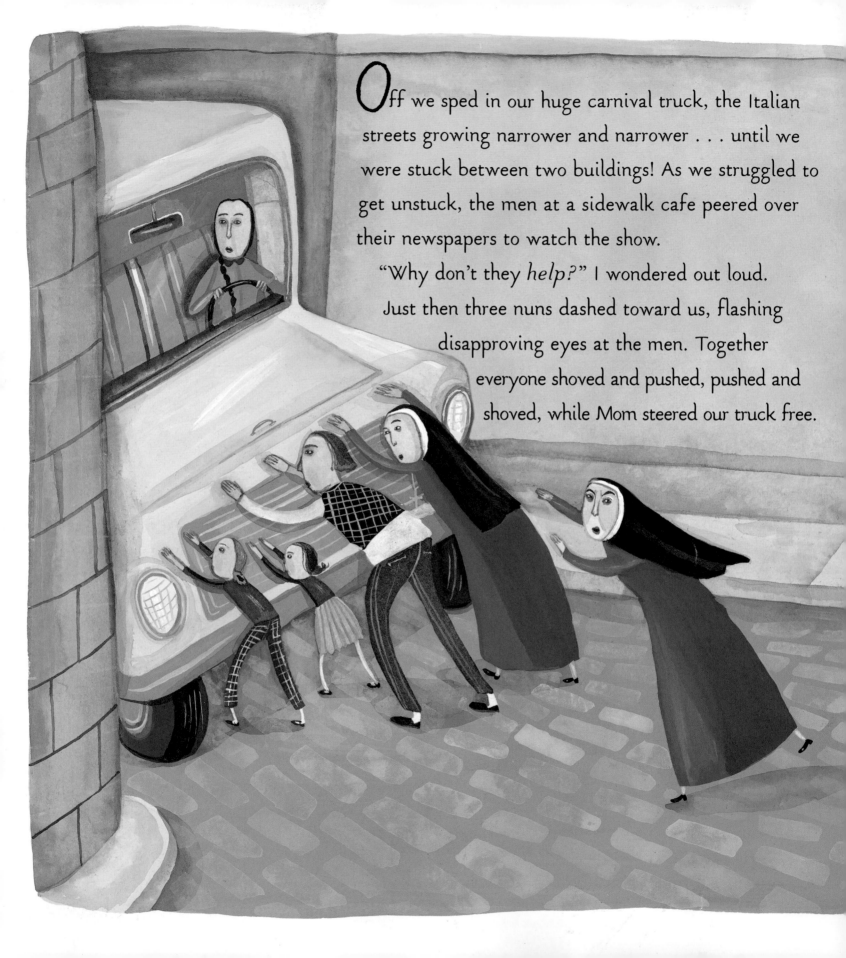

Off we sped in our huge carnival truck, the Italian streets growing narrower and narrower . . . until we were stuck between two buildings! As we struggled to get unstuck, the men at a sidewalk cafe peered over their newspapers to watch the show.

"Why don't they *help?*" I wondered out loud. Just then three nuns dashed toward us, flashing disapproving eyes at the men. Together everyone shoved and pushed, pushed and shoved, while Mom steered our truck free.

I wrote in my journal:

THE TRUCK is on it's WAY!
HAVE YOU ANYThing to SAY?
HURRAY, HURRAY!
The NUNS have SAVED the DAY,
And NOW WE'LL DO OUR PLAY!

THE
Mystic PaPer
BEASTS

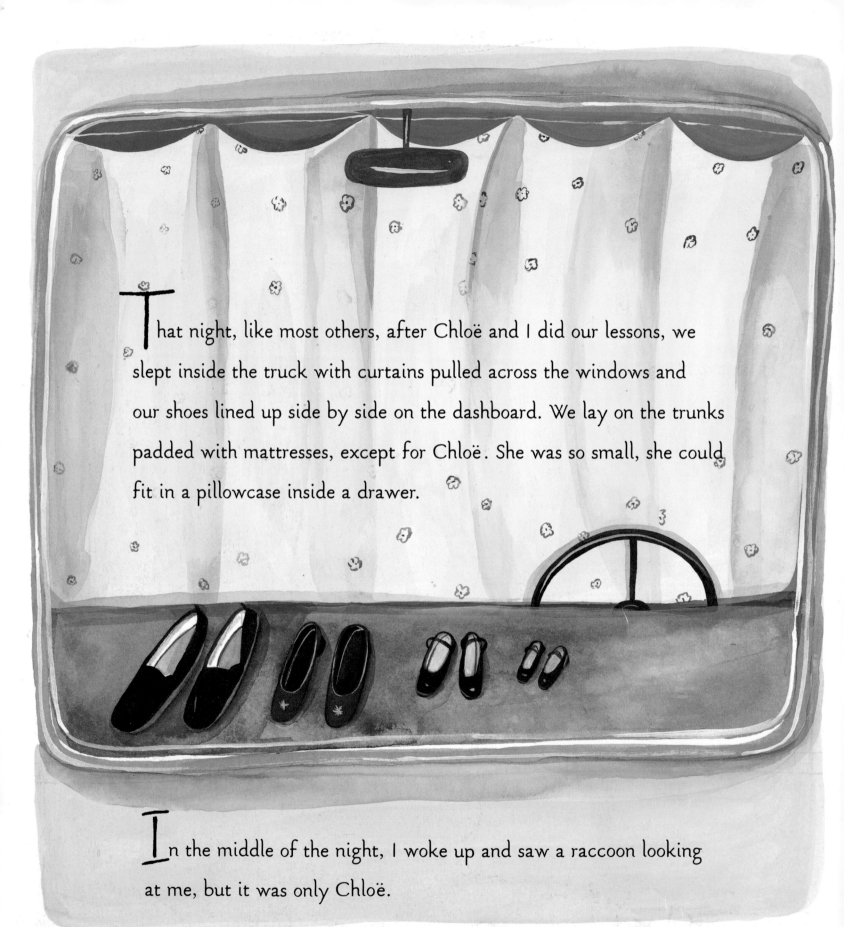

That night, like most others, after Chloë and I did our lessons, we slept inside the truck with curtains pulled across the windows and our shoes lined up side by side on the dashboard. We lay on the trunks padded with mattresses, except for Chloë. She was so small, she could fit in a pillowcase inside a drawer.

In the middle of the night, I woke up and saw a raccoon looking at me, but it was only Chloë.

Our next stop was Spoleto, a town perched above a deep valley, where we stayed in a house full of circus people. There was Eva, who could hang by her long hair and play the tuba; Pesia, who ate fire; Pepito, a parrot who cried like a baby; Silvano, who taught me and Chloë how to do a back-flip; and a tiny man named Hans, who always made jokes I didn't understand.

In town was a tiny building that had once been a church, and that's where we performed. My first role was as a bird that introduced my parents' act. I hated to speak in front of crowds, especially in other languages, but I could say anything behind a mask. "Il Ballo Matrimoniale d'Uccelli!" I twittered, which means, "The Wedding Dance of the Birds!"

On cue, Mom, a white dove in a wedding veil, floated in, playing the whistle and admiring herself in a mirror.

Dad, a dodo bird, offered her gifts—a giant worm and a tiny house—that she refused. Finally he offered her the world, which she happily accepted, and they waltzed away.

Then Mom swooped back, carrying an enormous golden egg, and *pop!* out came her two baby birds, whistling and fluttering.

After every show, Dad would announce, "Now, we will pass the hat!" That's when Chloë and I would flutter into the audience with hats to collect money.

"Grazie, grazie," we'd chirp over and over.

I loved counting the heavy foreign coins with Dad. "Enough for dinner," he'd say, and we'd all head off to eat.

The restaurants in Italy had paper tablecloths to draw on and bread you could roll up into little balls. I always ate spaghetti with a fried egg on top, while I watched people eating and laughing, their hands swirling in the air just like my grandfather Fuller.

On the tablecloth I made a list of the words I had learned in Italian:

IO sono Gisella

Panda

i spAghetti con BURRO

uovo al tegame

UCCELLi

gelato

Due BAMBINE

SCARPE

CiAO!

Our next stop was Assisi, a town that looks like a hat on a hill. We ate roasted chestnuts in newspaper cones, and Mom bought me and Chloë each a pair of cowboy boots. They were stiff and smelled smoky. As we marched proudly around the piazza, all the pigeons flew up at our stomping command.

Then suddenly I heard, "Yelp, Rrrrr, Yip, Rrrrr, yip!" followed by "AAAAAaaaaaaaaahhhhhhh!"

A dog the color of dirty water had bitten Chloë. I guess she'd been watching her boots too much and stepped right on the dog's tail. Mom wrapped Chloë up in her coat and rocked her crying away. Chloë had to get a rabies shot in a scary, green hospital.

One afternoon while we were having a picnic, Chloë and I found a shiny, red purse. I put it over my shoulder and wiggled my hips from side to side like a fancy lady. "Signore y signori, look at my new purse!" I shouted. But inside we found a card with "Signora Carlotta" printed on it, and an address. Mom made us track the card person down and return her purse. Carlotta was so happy that she invited us to a party at her pizza garden. We ate little pizzas with thin crusts until our bellies puffed up, and watched people dancing under the sparkly lights.

Rome was our last stop. Late late at night we performed in an open-air theater in the rain. When it was time for Chloë to be a monkey . . .

"Where's Chloë?" Mom asked.

"Where's Chloë?" Dad whisper-yelled, his eyes wide.

Under the pile of bird masks, peacock feathers, cloth worms, and a wedding dress, I found her asleep in her monkey costume, holding a smashed banana. "Quick, wake up!" I whispered, shaking her, and pushed her onstage where the lights were bright and the audience was a sea of scary, black umbrellas.

She ran backstage again, sobbing.

Mom whispered quick, panicky words to me, and suddenly I was onstage, wearing Chloë's tiny monkey mask upside down, still hot and wet with tears, . . . feeling dizzy, and doing somersaults without being able to see.

But now it was time for the grande finale.

"Hold on to the edge of your seats, folks! Before your very eyes I will tame two fierce, angry lions to be as harmless as sweet little girls!" Dad announced as he cracked his whip.

And guess who appeared? Chloë, her tears dried, leaped through his hoop and clawed at the air, making tiny roars. I was right behind.

Dad swept us up onto his shoulders and we removed our masks. Ta-da!

Always smile when you bow. I heard Dad's words in my head. Afterward a woman with bright lips gave Chloë and me a box of pastries. "You are the smallest, bravest actresses I have ever seen!" she gushed. We felt shy and proud at the same time.

The night before we went home, I couldn't sleep. I had gotten used to our big, old truck and waking up in my funny bed to see a different place out the window every morning. I would miss smelling new smells and eating gelato. School, so far away, seemed boring and hard. I couldn't wait to see Alice and Fuller, but what if they didn't even recognize me?

But there they were, waving as we got off the plane.
Fuller took off his hat and danced a funny greeting dance
with tears in his eyes, and Alice hugged me tight.

It almost seemed like I had never left until I looked down at my cowboy boots and thought of all the places they had been.

Latte CALDO  Hot Milk

SPAghetti Al BuRRO

CAIO   Bye-Kli

Due BAMBini

DOMANI SeRA tommorow evening

UOVO   FRITE

PANe

SCARPi

CAPELLO

IO Sono Gisella I am Giselle

HOWE LIBRARY
13 E. SOUTH ST.
HANOVER, N.H. 03755

SOLDi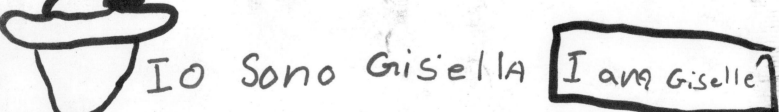

OCT 4 2002